Local Government
BOARD
BUILDERS

Strategic Planning for Elected Officials

Second Edition

Obed Pasha

**School of
Government**

The School of Government at the University of North Carolina at Chapel Hill works to improve the lives of North Carolinians by engaging in practical scholarship that helps public officials and citizens understand and improve state and local government. Established in 1931 as the Institute of Government, the School provides educational, advisory, and research services for state and local governments. The School of Government is also home to a nationally ranked Master of Public Administration program, the North Carolina Judicial College, and specialized centers focused on community and economic development, information technology, and environmental finance.

As the largest university-based local government training, advisory, and research organization in the United States, the School of Government offers up to 200 courses, webinars, and specialized conferences for more than 12,000 public officials each year. In addition, faculty members annually publish approximately 50 books, manuals, reports, articles, bulletins, and other print and online content related to state and local government. The School also produces the *Daily Bulletin Online* each day the General Assembly is in session, reporting on activities for members of the legislature and others who need to follow the course of legislation.

Operating support for the School of Government's programs and activities comes from many sources, including state appropriations, local government membership dues, private contributions, publication sales, course fees, and service contracts.

Visit sog.unc.edu or call 919.966.5381 for more information on the School's courses, publications, programs, and services.

Aimee N. Wall, DEAN
Jeffrey B. Welty, SENIOR ASSOCIATE DEAN FOR FACULTY AFFAIRS
Anita R. Brown-Graham, ASSOCIATE DEAN FOR STRATEGIC INITIATIVES
Willow S. Jacobson, ASSOCIATE DEAN FOR GRADUATE STUDIES
Kara A. Millonzi, ASSOCIATE DEAN FOR RESEARCH AND INNOVATION
Lauren G. Partin, SENIOR ASSOCIATE DEAN FOR ADMINISTRATION
Sonja Matanovic, ASSOCIATE DEAN FOR STRATEGIC COMMUNICATIONS
Matt Marvin, ASSOCIATE DEAN FOR ADVANCEMENT AND PARTNERSHIPS

FACULTY

Whitney Afonso
Gregory S. Allison
Rebecca Badgett
Julie Beasley
Maureen Berner
Kirk Boone
Mark F. Botts
Brittany LaDawn Bromell
Melanie Y. Crenshaw
Crista M. Cuccaro
Leisha DeHart-Davis
Shea Riggsbee Denning
Sara DePasquale
Kimalee Cottrell Dickerson
Phil Dixon, Jr.
Belal Elrahal
Rebecca L. Fisher-Gabbard
Jacquelyn Greene

Timothy Heinle
Cheryl Daniels Howell
Joseph L. Hyde
Colt Jensen
James L. Joyce
Robert P. Joyce
Diane M. Juffras
Joseph Laizure
Kirsten Leloudis
Adam Lovelady
James M. Markham
Christopher B. McLaughlin
Jill D. Moore
Jonathan Q. Morgan
Taylor Morris
Ricardo S. Morse
C. Tyler Mulligan
Kimberly L. Nelson

Kristi A. Nickodem
Obed Pasha
William C. Rivenbark
John Rubin
Dylan Russell
Meredith Smith
Daniel Spiegel
Carl W. Stenberg III
John B. Stephens
Elliot Stoller
Charles Szypszak
Shannon H. Tufts
Amy Wade
Teshanee T. Williams
Catherine Wilson
Kristina M. Wilson

Printed in the United States of America
29 28 27 26 25 25   1 2 3 4 5
ISBN 978-1-64238-131-3

About the Series

Local Government Board Builders offers local elected leaders practical advice on how to effectively lead and govern. Each of the booklets in this series provides a topic overview, and many offer specific tips on effective practice, worksheets, and reflection questions to help local elected leaders improve their work. The series focuses on common activities for local governing boards, such as selecting and appointing committees and advisory boards, planning for the future, making better decisions, improving board accountability, and effectively engaging stakeholders in public decisions.

Other Books in This Series

Leading Your Governing Board: A Guide for Mayors and County Board Chairs, Vaughn Mamlin Upshaw, 2009

A Model Code of Ethics for North Carolina Local Elected Officials, A. Fleming Bell, II, 2010

Creating and Maintaining Effective Local Government Citizen Advisory Committees, Vaughn Mamlin Upshaw, 2010

Working with Nonprofit Organizations, Margaret Henderson, Lydian Altman, Suzanne Julian, Gordon P. Whitaker, and Eileen R. Youens, 2010

Public Outreach and Participation, John B. Stephens, Ricardo S. Morse, and Kelley T. O'Brien, 2011

Local Government Revenue Sources in North Carolina, Kara A. Millonzi, 2011

Getting the Right Fit: The Governing Board's Role in Hiring a Manager, Vaughn Mamlin Upshaw, John A. Rible IV, and Carl W. Stenberg, 2011

The Property Tax in North Carolina, Christopher B. McLaughlin, 2012

Local Government Budgeting: A Guide for North Carolina Elected Officials, Julie M. Brenman with Gregory S. Allison, 2013

Handbook for North Carolina Mayors and Council Members, David M. Lawrence, 2013

How Are We Doing? Evaluating Manager and Board Performance, Vaughn Mamlin Upshaw, 2014

Wicked Problems: What Can Local Governments Do? Eric M. Reese and Maureen M. Berner, 2014

Suggested Rules of Procedure for the Board of County Commissioners, Joseph S. Ferrell, Third Edition, 2002

Suggested Rules of Procedure for Small Local Government Boards, A. Fleming Bell, II, Second Edition, 1998

Suggested Rules of Procedure for a City Council, A. Fleming Bell, II, Third Edition, 2000.

Acknowledgments

This edition of *Strategic Planning for Elected Officials* builds on the previous version, authored by Lydian Altman, Margaret Henderson, and Vaughn Mamlin Upshaw, and published in 2017.

Contents

What Is Strategic Planning?

Strategic planning is a process through which an organization's leaders agree on what the organization is, identify a desired future state, and organize their resources and efforts toward meeting the desired future state. A strategic plan is a dream for your community and a promise to realize that dream. It offers a collectively agreed-upon vision to work toward. Figure 1 represents the three big questions that strategic planning helps answer.

Figure 1. Three Big Questions of Strategic Planning

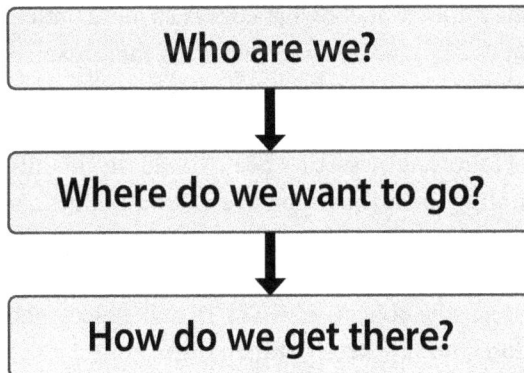

Who are we?

↓

Where do we want to go?

↓

How do we get there?

There are many ways to design strategic plans, and the best design process for you depends on the needs of your organization and your community. At a minimum, a good plan provides a long-term vision of what people want their community to look like and identifies five to eight broad goals that will move the community toward that vision.

Figure 2. Strategic Plan Framework

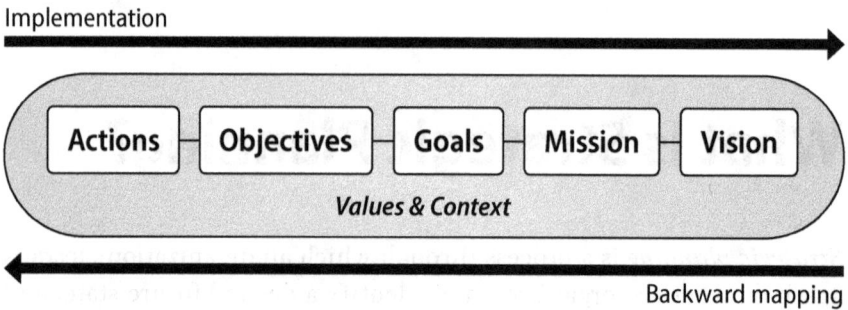

Implementation

Actions — Objectives — Goals — Mission — Vision

Values & Context

Backward mapping

The Strategic Plan Framework

Figure 2 presents the strategic plan framework, consisting of values, context, vision, mission, goals, objectives, and actions. Values, mission, and context help define who we are. Vision helps define where we want to be. Goals, objectives, and actions help define how we will get there.

Values set the foundation for what counts as moral, ethical, and acceptable behavior in your organization. *Context* is the organization's internal and external environmental realities.

In the strategic planning process, we begin by developing the vision and mission. This is followed by setting goals based on the mission, defining objectives that align with those goals, and finally outlining the actions needed to achieve these objectives. This approach is known as backward mapping. When it comes to implementing the strategic plan, we start with actions that advance the objectives, which in turn help to achieve the goals, fulfill the mission, and ultimately realize the vision.

The *vision* articulates the desired future state. A compelling vision statement should inspire employees, stakeholders, and residents. It should describe what success looks like, both internally and externally, and capture the public entity's long-term aspirations. The *mission* defines why an organization, department, or other public entity exists and what its overarching purpose is. An effective mission statement should be memorable, providing a clear sense of direction for the employees and their stakeholders. *Goals* help pinpoint the most pressing issues, challenges, and opportunities that require attention. *Objectives* help operationalize those

Table 1. Components of a Strategic Plan and the Questions They Answer

Component	Definition
Context	• What are our strengths, weaknesses, opportunities, and threats? • What do we expect to change in our environment? • What do we expect to remain the same?
Values	• How do we want to treat others? • How do we expect to be treated by others? • What are we (not) willing to do to achieve our purpose? • What principles are embedded in our code of conduct? • What are our moral and ethical foundations?
Vision	• What should the organization look like in the future? • What do we want the future to look like? • What do the community and environment look like if we fulfill our mission and values?
Mission	• Why does our organization exist? • What does it do and why do we do it? • What is its purpose?
Goals	• What are the most pressing issues that we are facing? • What areas do we need to address to fulfill our mission? • What needs our attention the most to meet our mission?
Objectives	• How can we operationalize the goals? • What criteria of success will we use to demonstrate the achievement of our goals?
Actions	• How will we mitigate weaknesses and threats? • How will we capitalize on strengths and opportunities? • How will we meet the stated objectives? • How will we address strategic issues?

goals by setting criteria for success. *Actions* are the activities that move the needle on the objectives. See Table 1 for questions to consider while developing each of the framework components.

Strategic Planning in Performance Management

Strategic plans are most effective when they are implemented as part of the broader performance-management system. Their codified mission, goals, and objectives provide performance-management systems with purpose,

Figure 3. The Performance-Management Cycle

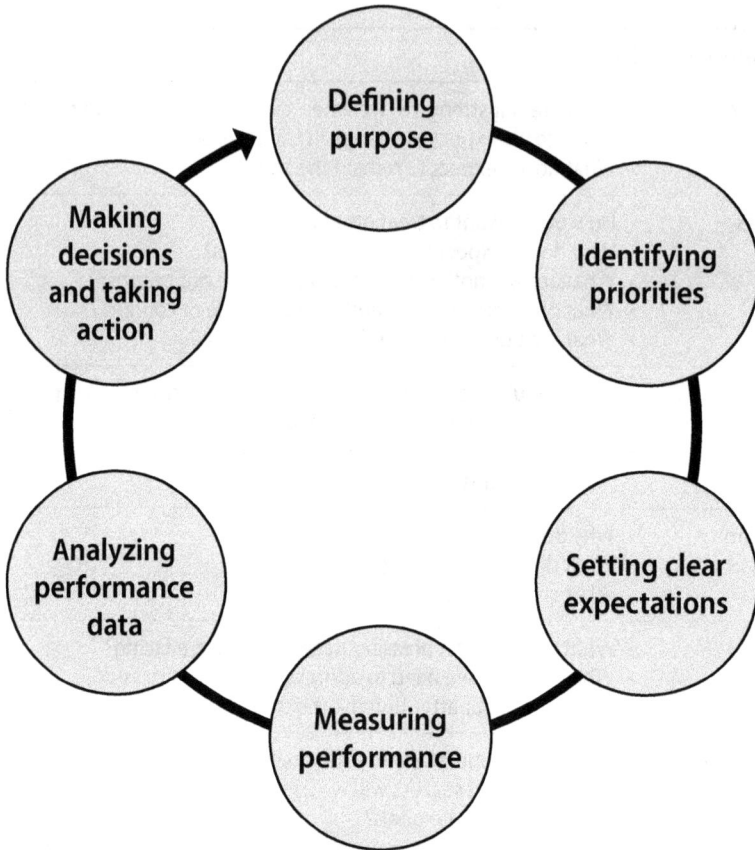

priorities, and expectations. The performance-management system measures progress in achieving objectives and goals and enables managers to adjust the strategic actions defined in the plan to better accomplish the organization's purpose.

Figure 3 presents the performance-management cycle: defining the organizational purpose, identifying priorities, setting clear expectations for managers, measuring progress toward the organization's objectives, analyzing performance data, and making evidence-informed decisions and taking actions to fulfill the organizational purpose.

Why Plan?

Strategic planning empowers elected board members to help transform their aspirations into actionable outcomes by crafting and communicating a shared vision for the community. This vision invites collective participation and shared responsibility from elected leaders, management, and staff.

The strategic plan helps define and articulate the board's vision and goals. It clarifies to the middle managers, supervisors, and frontline employees what the board expects from them. Plans also help communicate the board's goals to members of the community.

Additionally, strategic plans help ensure that all organizational activities are aligned with the board's priorities, particularly in addressing challenges and leveraging opportunities. It identifies the actions that will make progress toward the goals that will produce the desired results.

Without shared goals, stakeholders are more likely to divide, displace, and contend over resources in pursuit of their individual short-term interests rather than tackling the larger issues that extend beyond any individual's term in office. An elected board member's short-term promises may sometimes conflict with a governing board's long-term goals, but all elected officials benefit when they can point to how they are making progress on those goals.

Finally, strategic plans can offer stability and a sense of continuity as community leaders move, retire, and shift roles in local government, offering a foundation on which new leaders can develop a new vision.

What Role Do Elected Officials Play in Strategic Planning?

A strategic plan provides a focus to guide decisions and actions related to resource allocation, policy development, accountability, and transparency. It can be particularly valuable to public leaders who want to be forward-thinking and to build consensus on the direction and intent of long-term initiatives to improve their communities.

Elected board members can initiate discussions with the manager or suggest that the organization develop a strategic plan. However, in those communities using the council-manager form, *the decision to engage in strategic planning rests with the municipal or county manager* since the manager and staff are responsible for all organizational operations.

Arguably, the most important role of an elected body is to set the vision for a community. The support and involvement of the elected board is crucial to strategic planning: through the work involved in the planning process, such as making decisions on investments in public infrastructure or creating policies about land use, the board provides the big-picture vision for an organization and a community. If the governing board does not support the planning process, there is no reason to invest resources in the work. Only when the elected officials are committed to strategic planning will the efforts be sustained over time.

Supportive elected leaders openly communicate their vision and desires for the community. Sometimes, it can be challenging for the manager, supervisors, and frontline employees to ascertain what the board expects of them. Elected leaders should participate in all opportunities such as surveys, focus groups, and other discussions to share their vision.

Supportive elected leaders take time to understand the context of what is happening locally, regionally, nationally, and globally and to ask how these changes will affect their communities over time. There is much we do not know about the future, but some facts we know to be true: the world around us is changing. It will not remain static or return to the way it once was. Information about a community's past patterns and present context is crucial to shaping its future.

> **Elected leaders must ask the following questions to make sure that they are ready to engage in the strategic planning process:**
>
> - Are we ready to actively participate in the strategic planning process by communicating our vision and goals for the community?
> - Are we ready to listen to organizational supervisors and frontline employees and to incorporate their vision and goals into the strategic plan?
> - Are we ready to listen to and engage with external stakeholders?
> - Are we ready to learn and are we open to changing our position in light of new information?
> - Are we ready to make transformational changes to the organization and the community?
> - Are we ready to provide the resources needed to develop and implement the strategic plan?
> - Are we ready to use the strategic plan to guide our decision-making?

Supportive elected leaders use strategic planning to thoughtfully engage others as they work to improve the quality of community life over time. Most communities face issues that are persistent, difficult to identify, and felt across various sectors of the population. These problems cannot be solved by any one sector, organization, or leader. It takes the focus and commitment of elected leaders to engage with the community, each other, other governments, and the staff to make progress on such issues.

Supportive elected leaders are ready to allow and encourage transformational changes. Unlike private sector organizations that can pick up and move if the going gets rough, municipalities and counties must stay put. Disengaging, denying the realities, or ignoring trends is not an option for local governments. Elected leaders can make the difference by stepping up to highlight these issues and support the required changes to address them.

Supportive elected leaders provide the resources needed to implement the strategic plan. Developing a strategic plan is not enough. The true benefits of the strategic plan are realized when the organization's employees use it to make decisions and take action. It is essential that elected leaders understand and commit to aligning resources with stated goals.

Supportive elected leaders hold themselves and others accountable. Once a strategic plan is adopted, leaders throughout the organization must hold themselves accountable to achieve defined goals. The board does this by aligning its decisions with the strategic plan and empowering managers to make progress toward accomplishing their vision for the community.

Preparing for the Planning Process

Once elected board members are confident of their readiness to start planning, the next step is to help the municipal or county manager answer the following questions:

Why and how do we want to engage in strategic planning? Individual board members may hold many different motivations and expectations to create a strategic plan. Seeing and hearing their different purposes can help leaders identify common interests. Clarifying why strategic planning benefits your community and organization is a prerequisite to moving forward.

How far into the future do we want to plan? How might our plan accommodate short- and long-term goals? Some organizations may choose to integrate strategic planning into annual work plans. For example, following an annual planning retreat with elected officials, the town manager allocates resources toward meeting the strategic priorities set at the retreat and then, throughout the year, updates the governing board on the town's progress toward those goals. Other organizations could decide to formulate a long-range vision of five to ten years and then create a near-term plan (two to three years) for achieving that vision.

How broadly does our vision reach? Elected board members should consider the scope of their efforts. Typically, there are three levels of scope for a plan: the issue or project level, the organizational level, and the community level.

Who will facilitate the project? Determine who is going to direct the work. Consider whether there is internal capacity within the organization to undertake the effort or whether an external facilitator is needed. The choice of whether to use a consultant or external facilitator should happen before too much discussion about your objectives takes place. An external facilitator can provide valuable guidance and assistance to the planning group to design the work, assess needs, and make other planning decisions. Yet securing a trained facilitator will take time, effort, and money. Alternatives to engaging a trained facilitator are to look internally for someone with the desired skills or to seek volunteers from within the community. Some resources for finding external support include area councils of governments, community colleges, state agencies, and cooperative extension offices.

Who should be involved in the planning process? Local leaders are usually interested in incorporating some sort of community or stakeholder input into their strategic planning but are unclear on the extent of involvement they desire and what will be done. The choice of stakeholders depends on which stakeholders need to be involved. The scope of the leaders' vision will influence the design of the planning process. An all-encompassing community vision is best developed by involving a wide range of community stakeholders, like representatives of public and private sector organizations and people who live, work, worship, shop, and play in the community. Alternatively, a vision to address a single critical issue or project, such as workforce preparedness, will involve a narrower set of participants, like employers, educational institutions, or community-development agencies.

How Much Public Engagement Is Enough?

Sometimes, elected leaders become highly optimistic about opportunities to seek and incorporate public input. Efforts like this are a great way of seeking out valuable perspectives and generating interest in community change. Frustration and skepticism within the community are likely to result if the leaders say, "We are creating this plan with and for you" but do not allow opportunities for input or cocreation of the plan. On the other hand, higher public engagement is more resource-intensive and takes longer to develop consensus.

Elected leaders and managers can look into ways to seek public input without overburdening the system. Citizen advisory committees, for example, can be a good source of information about the community's priorities and interests.

Another strategy could be to focus on expanding educational opportunities that help residents learn about the many programs and services offered by their local governments. Residents' education can demonstrate the breadth and value of what gets done by local government, informing them about topics that are often overlooked or have a technical tilt, such as why water lines need to be repaired or replaced periodically or how the wastewater-treatment plant works. Such engagement could elicit better-informed suggestions from community members who participate.

Fostering Support for the Planning Process

Once the scope and process have been defined, the elected board should play its role in fostering broad-based support for the process. They can generate support in the following ways:

Defining Success

By defining what "success" and "progress" look like, elected leadership enables the local government manager to organize the planning process. The elected board can begin to define success by identifying the expected outcomes of the strategic planning process.

Providing Space for Discussions

Effective strategic planning requires all stakeholders to openly share their experiences, values, and vision for the organization. Elected leaders should help provide space for participants, especially employees, to feel safe while sharing their opinions even if those opinions conflict with those of the elected board.

Encouraging Participation from the Front Lines

The elected board should encourage the manager to include middle managers, supervisors, and frontline staff in all discussions since they are the ones responsible for implementing the plan.

Embracing Ambiguity

For strategic planning to be effective and inclusive, elected leaders should agree on the overall direction and scope of the process while permitting new opportunities and previously unrecognized issues to be considered and incorporated into the plan as the process develops. Discussions may sometimes be complex, and interests can seem to conflict as participants express various perspectives.

?

Elected leaders can consider the following questions to help foster support for the strategic planning process:

- Why do we want to engage in strategic planning?
- What are we planning for (an organization, the community, the region, or something else)?
- Who has a stake in our strategic plan? Who will our planning affect? Who will affect our long-term success?
- If our process is successful, how will things be different five years from now?
- How much staff, money, time, and other resources will we commit to our planning effort?

Developing the Plan

As a rule of thumb, if an organization already has a strategic plan, start with an environmental analysis, such as SWOT (strengths, weaknesses, opportunities, and threats), based on the existing mission statement to determine what might be helping or hindering the fulfillment of the organization's purpose. Then review the mission, followed by the vision, values, goals, objectives, and actions. If an organization has never had a strategic plan, start with developing a mission statement to define the purpose of the organization, followed by the environmental analysis based on the mission. Then define the organization's vision, values, goals, objectives, and actions.

As stated before, values, mission, and context help define *who we are*. Vision helps define *where we want to be*. Goals, objectives, and actions help define *how we will get there*. These three main questions of strategic planning guide the entire process.

Who Are We?

Values, mission, and context are the three components of the strategic plan that define the organization itself.

Values

Elected leaders help determine the values of the organization by setting criteria for what behavior is acceptable, unacceptable, encouraged, and discouraged. They also offer their insight into how they expect the organization and its employees to treat the community's residents and visitors.

As representatives of their community, elected officials should consider the values they believe are important to members of the community when making decisions. This is one reason for engaging in a values exercise as part of the strategic planning process. Ideally, a government organization will embody the values of the community as expressed by elected officials.

? **Facilitation questions**

- How should the government's staff and elected officials conduct themselves?
- How should we treat our residents?
- What standards and practices for the treatment of our employees should we adopt?
- What core values should we adhere to?

Mission

During the portion of the strategic planning process devoted to articulating the government's mission, elected leaders describe what they consider the core purpose of the organization to be. The perceived purpose of the organization can vary among the elected members and even contradict the supervisors' and frontline employees' own perceptions. Elected leaders should be open to listening to employees and should develop a shared understanding of organizational purpose through persuasion and negotiation.

? **Facilitation question**

How would you complete these sentences?

- Our town/city/county government exists to . . .
- The core purpose of our local government is to . . .

Context (SWOT Analysis)

To make informed decisions about goals for the local government, it is important to first consider the context in which the government is operating at the time of the plan. In addition, contextual analysis will attempt to anticipate those future challenges and opportunities that are on the horizon.

There are multiple frameworks to use to engage in a contextual analysis. The two most common are the SWOT and SOAR methods. Governments that are highly resourced may contract with an independent organization to collect data for the analysis or may use internal data.

Regardless of the method used for data collection, elected leaders should use that data to identify current and near-future prospects and challenges for the organization or community. In this part of the strategic planning process, elected leaders will share their perspective on internal and external threats and opportunities.

? **Facilitation questions**

- What key internal strengths enable us to effectively pursue our mission?
- What key internal weaknesses prevent us from fulfilling our mission?
- What external opportunities may help us fulfill our mission?
- What external threats may prevent us from fulfilling our mission?

Where Do We Want to Be?

After reaching an understanding about the environment in which the local government operates and developing a shared understanding of the mission and values of the organization, the next step in the process is to reach consensus about the vision for the organization and/or community.

Elected leaders play the most significant role in developing the vision. Elected board members help develop community vision by imagining a desired future for the community. Individual members offer their respective visions for the organization and the community and consider the visions of other important stakeholders. An expert facilitator can help synthesize these disparate visions and bring them back to the elected board for review and approval. Ideally, this process uncovers commonalities among participants and begins to create networks for change.

? **Facilitation question**

How would you complete these sentences?

- Ten years from now, I want our town/city/county to be . . .
- Ten years from now, I want our town/city/county to have . . .
- Ten years from now, I would like our town/city/county to be recognized for . . .

How Will We Get There?

Goals

The values, mission, and vision guide the development of the strategic plan's goals. At this point, many local governments increase the role of the management and staff in the process.

The role of elected representatives in setting goals is to offer what they consider to be the main priorities for the organization as it fulfills its mission and vision. Organizations typically set five to eight internal and external goals. Internal goals refer to organizational improvement, such as strengthening human resources, finances, or processes; external goals refer to improving service effectiveness and efficiency.

? Facilitation questions

- What must we achieve to benefit from our strengths and manage our weaknesses?
- What must we achieve to benefit from the opportunities and mitigate the challenges of the next five years?
- What must we achieve to successfully fulfill the mission and vision of our local government?
- What results does a high-performing local government achieve?
- What impact does a high-performing local government have?

Objectives

To be able to evaluate progress on achieving strategic planning goals, staff will identify measurable objectives that are matched to the goals. It is essential that these objectives be measurable, time-bound, and challenging. The elected board may negotiate with the manager to adjust the criteria to make sure that the criteria meet its expectations and that they are ambitious without being discouraging.

? Facilitation questions

- What would progress toward this goal look like (for example: fewer of this, more of that)?
- What would the criteria be for determining whether the goal was fulfilled?

Actions

The responsibility for action lies with the managers, departments, divisions, and units. Elected representatives should offer their suggestions to the manager and ensure that the suggested actions are in line with the organization's values.

? Facilitation questions

- What actions can help move the needle on these objectives?
- What policies, practices, actions, or strategies could we adopt to make progress toward the objective?
- In a perfect world, what would we be able to do to fulfill our mission?

Assigning Champions

To increase the likelihood that goals and objectives are accomplished, the organization needs a specific work plan that outlines how the indicators of progress or success will be produced and who will be responsible for producing them. Responsibility for implementing changes will likely fall across multiple groups at all levels of the organization, starting with the management team and then moving down into multiple departments, units, and individuals. By sharing draft objectives with those who will be involved in carrying out the work, decision-makers get valuable input from the responsible groups and will describe more accurately how and when actions will occur and what results can be expected.

In this process, people at multiple levels of the organization need to answer these questions:

- What am I responsible for to make the vision a reality?
- What are others responsible for?
- How does our work fit together?

Goal champions can be middle managers or members of the leadership team who are assigned the responsibility of fulfilling the goal. These champions coordinate efforts and ensure that actions are appropriately sequenced so that they complement rather than compete with other expectations. These champions provide their team members the resources and the direction they need to further the goal. If there are too many objectives or if the work falls to only a limited number of people, efforts are likely to falter. Champions must make sure that the objectives are clearly tied to strategic goals and that the responsibility for action is appropriately distributed.

Allocating Resources

Once goals have been outlined in an action plan, elected leaders need to provide the resources and support necessary for successful implementation. Otherwise, the priorities they have identified will be forgotten and the effort will have been wasted. Only after the manager devises the work plan is it appropriate to move forward and allocate those resources. The elected board should work with the manager to ensure that everyone agrees on what should be done first, when it should be done, who should do it, and what measure should be used to monitor progress.

Resources can be in the form of people, equipment, expertise, time, or money. Some of the necessary resources might be in place or be easily redirected from a lesser priority. However, some goals may require a major reorganization of current resources (such as redesigning the way groups work together in a new effort) or a major attempt to gain new resources (such as a bond referendum to fund construction).

Resources are made available by the governing board and management through the annual budget. The resources needed to support both short- and long-term strategies often flow upward from departmental plans and budgeting processes. Some local governments use a capital-budgeting process to fund long-term strategies, often requiring substantial investments over time, such as building new facilities and infrastructure.

Selecting funding strategies can be difficult even in good economic times. No organization gets to do all that it wants. Winnowing the list of funded priorities becomes especially difficult in challenging economic times. In such situations, strategic plans can become incredibly useful to ensure that the activities aligned with organizational mission and vision are prioritized over the actions that may not be central to their achievement.

Measuring Progress

For many organizations, strategic planning occurs when management and board leaders hold a retreat and agree on a handful of goals. Some will take this a step further and use these goals to guide the annual budget process. Fewer local governments have created systems to monitor, measure, and evaluate results.

Too often, strategic goals get lost as leaders respond to crises or get swept up by newer, shinier ideas begging for attention. There will always be opportunities to pursue new projects and services that would benefit communities. Some of these may seem more interesting than monitoring and evaluating goals set months earlier during a planning retreat. If leaders stop paying attention to priorities, then others will too, and the strategic plan will fail.

Embedding strategic plans within performance management enables organizations and communities to begin with the end in mind. Taking time to measure, track, and assess progress provides leaders the opportunity to

- follow up on progress toward goals,
- translate big ideas into measurable goals and actions to ensure that staff and decision-makers are accountable,
- demonstrate accountability and stewardship by providing information to the public about progress,
- learn how best to strengthen the work, and
- celebrate the outcomes of successful efforts.

Elected leaders can support the performance management process in the following ways:

- If the staff or community brings accurate data forward, give it careful and full consideration, even if it does not support your current views.
- If innovations designed to improve results are proposed, consider making changes to the status quo.
- If performance statistics show improved performance, congratulate those who made it happen.
- If performance declines, indicate concern but listen respectfully to explanations and plans for improvement.

Making
Data-Informed Decisions

While strategic plans lay out what the organization needs to do in order to fulfill its mission, adjustments to these plans will, at times, be necessary. Unforeseen complications might arise. Unexpected opportunities might come up. Aspects of a new service or process might work beautifully in one neighborhood but not in another. To ensure that improvements occur continually and that learning is ongoing, elected leaders should emphasize honing future performance rather than assigning blame when expectations are not fully met.

In response to the evaluation of what has been accomplished and what has not turned out as planned, people within the organization should be encouraged to find and propose new ways of aligning internal or external programs, strategies, and resources to accomplish the desired goals. The internal discussion during this process provides an opportunity to explore possibilities for improving the plan and building capacity to accomplish the long-term vision. Governing boards should also reflect on how well their decisions and actions align with their goals and should set priorities for their own work going forward.

An analysis of the results is the only way to determine whether a plan is accomplishing what it was designed to achieve. This analysis entails collecting and reporting outcomes of the strategies put forth at the beginning of the year. Some results may seem small in comparison with the results for other strategic priorities. For instance, a project with the goal of building a new public facility may, by year's end, only have identified a way to fund the project, whereas a project with the goal of reducing crime rates may, as a result of smart policing and community engagement, end up outpacing itself. Either way, the work helps move the community or organization toward its vision. It is therefore wise to use quarterly, semiannual, and annual reports as a means of sharing both small and large achievements, keeping in mind that, by definition, strategic goals can take years to accomplish: if they were quick and easy, they wouldn't be called *strategic goals*; they'd be called a to-do list.

Making the Plan Successful

Many organizations consider the plan to be done once it has been developed and adopted by the elected body. A strategic plan is more likely to be successful when it is combined with other uses and purposes within an organization. Engaging and enabling multiple aspects of the organization provides much more leverage to move the organization, and the community, toward the desired future.

Successful boards, organizations, and communities have combined strategic planning with other practices in various ways. Measures of the plan's progress can be used as performance measures. The plan's priority goals can inform budgets and other resource-allocation decisions. Progress reports can be presented in a format that reflects the format of the strategic plan's documentation. Because a good strategic plan explains the organization's goals and the roles that employees play in reaching them, plan documentation can be a useful tool for recruiting, orienting, and motivating employees. The plan can also be a reference when making evidence-informed decisions during the performance-management cycle (see figure 3) if managers are encouraged to justify their decisions in terms of meeting the organization's goals, fulfilling its mission, and realizing its vision.

www.ingramcontent.com/pod-product-compliance
Lightning Source LLC
Chambersburg PA
CBHW071126210326
41519CB00020B/6442